Dark Mirror

For

my husband George

my children Anne, David and Eva

my grandchildren Soleil and Gino

and for my friends

Dark Mirror

Custom & Limited Editions ❧ San Francisco

Published by Custom & Limited Editions
41 Sutter Street, Suite #1634
San Francisco, California 94104
All rights reserved. No portion of this book may be
reproduced or used without the written permission of
the publisher.

Library of Congress Catalogue number 97-68571
ISBN 1-881529-23-1

Edited by Robert McDonald
Designed by Lilli Colton
Printed and bound in Italy

Permission to print a detail of "The Holocaust," 1982
by © George Segal, Collection of the City and County
of San Francisco, Commissioned by the Mayor's
Committee for a Memorial to the Six Million Victims
of the Holocaust, obtained from the artist's copyright
representative, VAGA, 521 5th Avenue, Suite 800,
New York, New York 10017

Dust jacket: "September 18"

In Dark Mirror Lisa Kanemoto presents a visual autobiography. Each image is like a chapter focusing on a crisis in her life. To compose her story she used a series of photographs, both straightforward and manipulated. The issues they portray are dramatic. Some are responses to major concerns of the western world during the past 60 years. Others are personal, yet parallel to those of many women everywhere. In this artist's work we see our epoch's history with a human face.

That face mirrors the events of both world history and personal biography: the Nazi dictatorship in Germany, the Holocaust, the death of an adored father on the Russian Front, the defeat of Germany in World War II, its occupation by ethnically diverse allied forces, marriage to a career army officer, children, the Cold War, periods of depression, the search for creative modes of self-expression, her son's mental illness, her own struggles with alcohol dependency and with breast cancer.

In making her photographs, Kanemoto thoroughly conceives and meticulously designs each image for a perfect economy of artistic process. She uses whatever techniques she feels are appropriate to their content and purpose, but especially montage, which so effectively imitates the workings of memory. Visual references are as ancient as the symbols identified by Carl Jung and as contemporary as the imagery of Pablo Picasso, Edvard Munch, Käthe Kollwitz and George Segal.

This book is a statement about the interconnectedness of all phenomena and an assertion of the necessity of creativity. Art is as essential to the spirit as water is to the body. Without art there is no life. In her being and her art Lisa Kanemoto offers us a piece of history. A mere speck, it has, nevertheless, an identity and a mission: They are both love.

—Robert McDonald, Editor

*I*f it's real, it's paradoxical, a wise woman once said to me. Silent, yet screaming. Lonely, yet engaged. Fragile, yet powerful. Still, yet moving. Dark, yet full of reflective light. These phrases describe some of the fused opposites, paradoxes, portrayed in this collection of Lisa Kanemoto's layered self-portraits. Photographic art is the channel through which her soul speaks.

Writing this introduction from the point of view of an art psychotherapist and artist, I have taken as my guide D.H. Lawrence's statement that, "The soul's deepest will is to preserve its own integrity, against the mind and the whole mass of disintegrating forces.... Soul sympathizes with soul." Lisa Kanemoto has survived the pain in her life by expressing herself in art. No other form of self-expression has worked for her so effectively as the healing process of creating photographs. She has allowed me to enter her life, her imagery; to experience once again the mystery of art's power to transform psychic destruction into psychic re-creation.

Reality and imagination collide in each photographic image appearing in Dark Mirror. There is a prevailing reality of associations in the superimpositions and reversals, that is, in the "surrealism" embraced in this body of work. Our emotions respond to a dynamic dialogue of tragic loss and resurrection between past and present, between present and future. We are seized by the dynamism and paralysis of a dreamlike state. The movement of this psychic storm carries us through Lisa Kanemoto's life story.

We enter her world of "Mourning."

She comes from Idar-Oberstein, a small town in Germany, where her father, like many others there, perfected his craft as a jeweler, shaping and etching metals, stones and gems into beautiful works of art. This idolized parent was lost in World War II fighting on the Eastern Front. Hiding in the shadows, her family concealed the secret of her mother's Jewish heritage. Lisa remembers her life changing completely, from then on feeling intense loneliness, grief, shyness and inferiority.

"My Father" portrays one of her last memories of her father in his uniform standing in a tunnel-like airplane hangar. Her hand reaches out to him. He disappeared in Russia, leaving her the object of the criticism, agitation and depressive emptiness of her widowed mother and aunt.

The Nazis decided her fate: a bitter "Nightmare" took her voice away pushing this shy girl into the group madness of "Sieg Heil," with forced participation in the Hitler Youth movement. Her choices were taken away; her hatred grew with each mandated raised arm.

She felt as "Branded" as the Jews who were marched through town each day, former neighbors and strangers forced into factory labor. This young girl identified with her Jewish friends who disappeared and with the bombing victims lying in the street. Observing destruction all around her, she responded to the various stresses she was experiencing by remaining mute. Growing up with intense survivor's "Guilt," feeling imprisoned by hatred and self-doubt, this girl emerged a tormented young woman, as we see in "Night" and "Finale."

As an adult, this survivor could not shake her despair. She learned and practiced the craft of goldsmith to honor her father. In 1958 she married a Japanese-American army officer who was part of the post-war occupation force in Germany. Her two daughters and a son gave her new life. After numerous moves throughout the United States and overseas, the family settled in San Francisco in 1975. Here Lisa sought meaning through painting and religion, but all expressions of self did not liberate her from the depth of her depression, her "Neurosis," or from her feelings of isolation and fear and her perfectionism.

As her bright and talented son "David" was about to begin his graduate studies, he was diagnosed with acute schizophrenia and became one of the chronically mentally ill for whom modern medicine has no cure. Another layer of tragedy had fallen on Lisa. Refuge in denial and alcohol could not console her for this loss.

Then a woman of forty-six, she turned to photography, an art form she had learned earlier while studying graphic art at Macomb Community College in Detroit. At City College of San Francisco, under the guidance of an inspiring photography teacher, Morrie Camhi, she discovered her real voice through the camera and a talent for photography. This teacher imparted compassion and understanding. She felt understood for the first time and stimulated to tell her inner truth.

Her sense of self was that of an "Outsider," and she began creating photographic essays about other outsiders: the developmentally disabled, the mentally ill, the gay and lesbian community and various ethnic populations living in the neighborhoods of San Francisco. Her empathy and love were mirrored in her subjects' photographs. The passion of her "Self-Analysis" was softened in her relationships to those she portrayed…. Souls meeting. The layering of past and present in her self-portraiture was becoming a liberating lament.

She alleviated bouts of depression by immersing herself in work. All of her questions about "What went wrong?" would fade into shadows. Her drive to create resurged. "Calm" became possible. Processing emotions through symbols permitted a transformation of sorrow and grief.

In some of the photographic images, the tree seems to act as a symbolic bridge between the Destructive Force (loss, guilt, despair, frustration, judgment, fall from divine grace, forbidden wisdom and death) and the Creative Force (beauty, generation, peace, greatness, health, organic unity, resurrection, refuge, knowledge and the family): as a narrow sky pillar in "Mourning," "Despair" and "Search"; as a massive, multi-figurative trunk in "The Marriage" and "Fate"; and as a cross in "Prayer" and "1984." The Sacred Tree, symbolized by a cross, is mirrored in the position of her arms and hands, especially in "September 18," "Denial" and "Mutilation." The Cosmic or World Tree, a strong life force, is often symbolized by a column or a torso. The Cosmic Tree, in Western and Eastern mythologies, births the Tree of Life and the Tree of Knowledge. In "Inhibition," "Dry Spell" and "The Diagnosis" we see the female torso, bound and still, paradoxically portraying a life force about to burst forth with the creative energy to endure. Symbolic processing at this intuitive level heals wounds so deep they may seem inaccessible. This dimension of human ability is soul medicine, maybe allowing this extraordinary woman to survive breast cancer, even after refusing the prescribed chemotherapy following surgery seven years ago.

The thorny branches wrapped around the face of "Mother" tell of the sacrifices that women make to sustain life in the face of death. Conflicts with nurturing and nurturance create neurosis and despair. But "The Poem," as a sacred gift offering from one woman to another, opens the heart and soul to song, to renewal. Opening to possibility is healing. Creative imagery that transforms layer upon layer of trauma is an expression of D.H. Lawrence's belief that "the soul's deepest will is to preserve its own integrity."

—Janet K. Long

There were joyous times, but I never had the desire to portray them. Instead, I was driven to explore my sorrows and torments and transform them into self-images. It gave me a sense of inner order, acceptance and peace.

—Lisa Kanemoto

Mourning

My Father

Nightmare

Branded

Sieg Heil

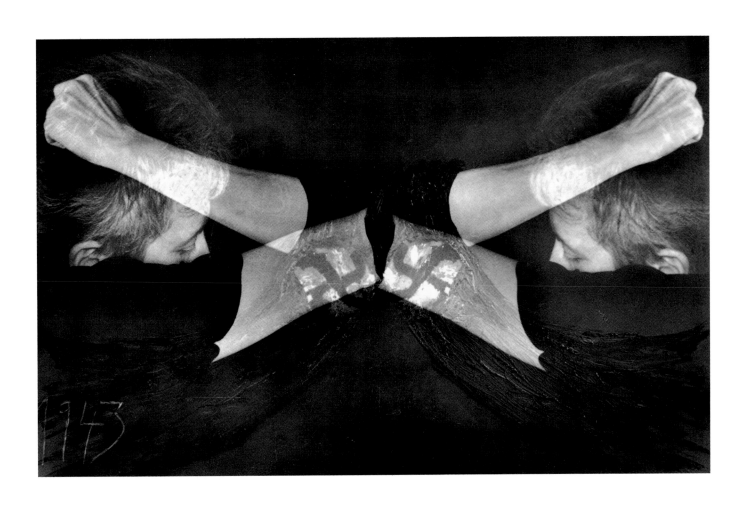

Night

Despair

Guilt

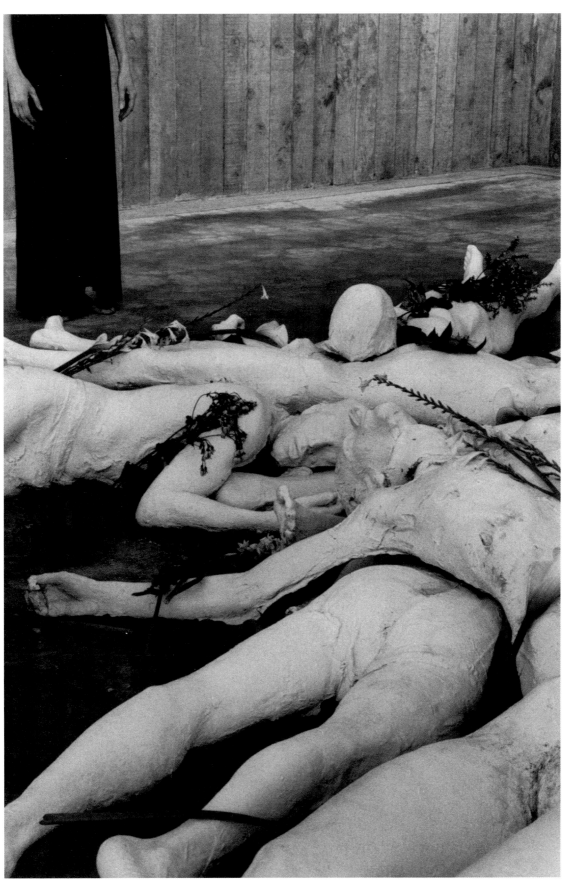

Identification

Finale

Rage

Masks

Self-Analysis

Selves

Neurosis

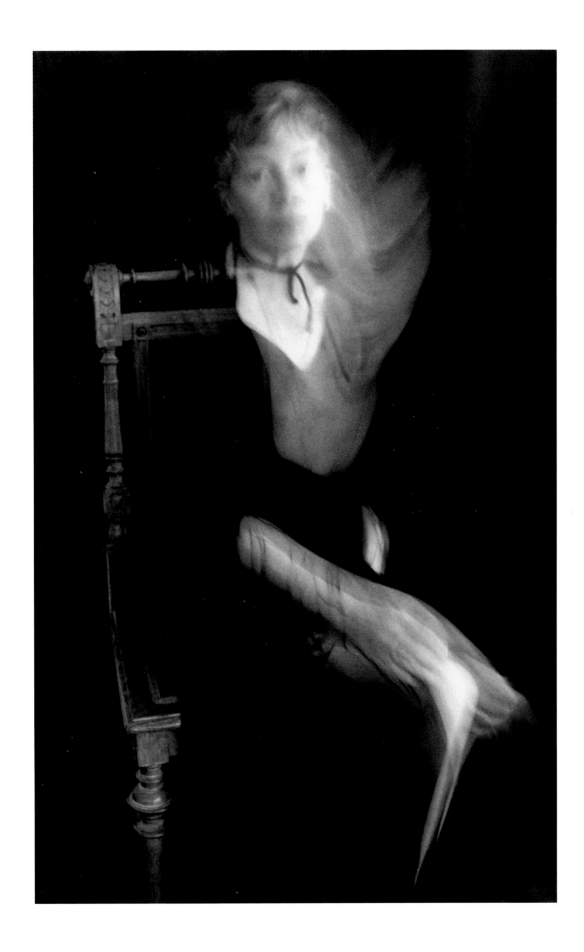

Prayer

Isolated

Outsider

Reflecting

Wretched

Self-Hate

Inhibition

September 18

The Marriage

Servant

Contemplation

David

Mother's Day

Anesthesia

Mother

Dry Spell

Calm

Search

Denial

1984

Aging

Angst

The Diagnosis

Mutilated

Mortality

Fate

The Poem

ACKNOWLEDGMENTS

A special thanks to my husband George, who so patiently tolerates my complexities and dark moods and supports and encourages me and stands by me in all I am doing.

I will be forever thankful to my friend Merit Philips for his interest and involvement in producing this book, for demonstrating a tireless enthusiasm for my projects and endeavors, for giving me the courage to realize my goals and for keeping our rare friendship alive.

A warm thank you to Morrie Camhi, my teacher and friend, for all the advice, words of wisdom and inspiration he has given me over the years and to Janet Long for helping to illuminate my images in her essay.

Working on the production of this book with a team as sensitive and caring as publisher Ron Fouts, editor Robert McDonald and designer Lilli Colton has been a comforting and joyful experience.

The gracious cooperation of the following organizations was essential to my creation of the images cited: the Holocaust Center of Northern California for a fabric Jewish star in "Branded"; the San Francisco Art Commission for a detail of George Segal's "The Holocaust" in "Guilt"; the City College of San Francisco for a detail of a sculpted wall in "Identification"; and the Exploratorium for a detail of an installation in "Masks."

I continue to be grateful to the National Endowment for the Arts, The Barbara Deming Memorial Fund and the Zellerbach Family Arts Committee.

——Lisa Kanemoto

Lisa Kanemoto lives in San Francisco, where she devotes her particular interest to "outsiders." Her photographs have been exhibited and published internationally and collected by institutions such as the Tokyo Metropolitan Museum of Photography, the Victoria and Albert Museum and the Bibliothèque Nationale. In 1982 she published *We Are,* a documentary monograph about San Francisco's gay and lesbian community. Her work-in-progress, *Against All Odds,* focuses on the stigma attached to mental illness.

Essayist **Janet K. Long**, A.T.R.-BC, M.F.C.C., an art psychotherapist and artist residing in Oakland, California, conducts a private practice with children and adults. She is Coordinator and Lead-Instructor of the Art Therapy Post-Masters Certificate Program at the University of California, Berkeley; Adjunct Professor at the California College of Arts and Crafts in Oakland and at Dominican College in San Rafael, California; and a Pain Management Specialist at Children's Hospital in Oakland.

Editor **Robert McDonald** is a former director of the de Saisset Museum of Santa Clara University and of The Art Museum of Santa Cruz County, a former Chief Curator of the Laguna Beach Museum of Art and of the La Jolla Museum of Contemporary Art, a *Los Angeles Times* art critic and a Contributing Editor of *Artweek.*

Lilli Colton is a freelance graphic designer residing in Southern California. With a background in art history and exhibitions, she works with museums and non-profit organizations on catalogues, posters and other publications.

❦ ❦ ❦

The images in *Dark Mirror* were produced between 1980 and 1995. The manuscript was edited by Robert McDonald. The book was designed by Lilli Colton and composed in Bernhardt Modern. 2000 copies were lithographed and bound in Italy.